*On Playing with Lions*

# On Playing with Lions

## VIRGINIA McKENNA
### and
## BILL TRAVERS

A HELEN AND KURT WOLFF BOOK
HARCOURT, BRACE & WORLD, INC.
NEW YORK

FOR ANNA, WILLIAM, LOUISE AND JUSTIN

# *Contents*

# Prologue
### by
### Virginia McKenna

The only times I had ever seen lions were at the circus or in zoos. My feelings towards them had been a combination of awe and pity —their magnificence and strength were indeed awe-inspiring but to what an undignified existence had they been subjected by humans —or should I say barbarians? This slight and objective awareness of these magnificent animals was to be violently catapulted into feelings of a very different kind—into friendship, into love.

It began over a tea-table at the Mayfair hotel in London—where Bill, my husband and I met two men concerned with the making of a film called *Born Free*. The men were the director and one of the producers and the story was about two people and a lioness—and their love for each other. We listened to them talk and we drank tea, but no amount of liquid could remove the dryness from our mouths or calm the thumping of our hearts. We never looked at each other, perhaps we hardly dared to for fear that our ill-concealed feelings of excitement were not mutual, as we listened, asked questions and waited for the one crucial question to be put to us 'Will you do it?'—'Yes'.

To the ordinary man and woman, life today offers few challenges —unless you fly in space or climb mountains or explore the silent world beneath the sea, one works to live to work again and few things interrupt the chain of events that lead from birth to death.

Here was a challenge indeed—not a test of strength or endurance, nor a race in which we had to be the winners—but the chance to find out whether we, as an actor and actress, as people with little knowledge of the ways of wild animals, could re-create truthfully and without tricks the story of Joy and George Adamson and Elsa their lioness. It was a wonderful story—here were people to believe in—ideals—beauty and love. A positive force for good.

Two-and-a-half months after the tea party we saw our first lions in Kenya. Ironically they were circus lions. It had been considered by many an impossible film to make—lions and actors just could not appear in the same scenes in close contact, but the people now attempting the film believed that somehow it could be done and they had decided that to play the full-grown Elsa they would use circus lions. Circus lions were predictable—they were trained—they were used, at least in one capacity, to human beings. They had been born or lived most of their lives in captivity and therefore it was supposed that as they had never killed or enjoyed a naturally wild life they would, of course, be less dangerous. We took this on good faith. The established pattern in the world of cinema was with circus animals. We were told briefly of other lions, Kenya- and Uganda-born, who had been considered for the part of Elsa, but they were thought to be too unreliable and unmanageable and dangerous. They had been used to varying degrees of human contact. Some had been found as small cubs, abandoned or lost by their mothers and taken to animal orphanages—some had been personal pets as small cubs and when they became too big to manage had been given, reluctantly I'm sure, into the care of these same orphanages.

It was a very bright and beautiful day—a Tuesday—with the snowy crown of Mount Kenya gazing benignly upon us and the air still and humming with insects. I saw the compounds ahead of me and I saw two large lionesses. They were very large. I think I talked and smiled—and Bill seemed to be doing the same—but I know my heart was thumping as it had two-and-a-half months before at the tea-table, and my mouth was drying up again. How could I ever go inside the compound with those animals? How *could* I? What on earth had I been dreaming of when I said I would try and get friendly with a lion, and stroke it and caress it and walk with it and swim with it? Was I mad? Obviously my tea-table answer applied here—'Yes'.

For five days we sat outside the compound—watching, listening, asking endless questions of Monika Gradischnig, the Austrian lion-trainer who was in charge of these two lions. We helped her prepare their food, helped her at feeding time, all the time helping ourselves to get used to our new workmates, and hoping they were getting used to us—our smell, our voices. What else were we hoping? Not to be loved, I think, perhaps not even to be accepted—perhaps just to be tolerated. It was all very strange. We thought by day and dreamed by night of lions. Even at this early stage we realized how impossible it would have been not to be doing this film together. Apart from the fact that our talk was 'lions', with only one person involved the conversation would have become rather limited—imagine how the one waiting at home would have felt knowing the other was inside the lions' cage. It doesn't bear imagining.

The tension mounted as the day when we would go into the cage grew nearer. On Monday morning Bill went in. Leather guards were put on his wrists, he was given two sticks to hold and he and Monika walked into the compound where Astra, the seven-year-old lioness was waiting. The training compound was roughly

$100 \times 80$ feet and surrounded by a 12 foot high thick wire mesh fence. At one end of it was a wooden house, built to represent the Adamson's home in the film and with which the lions had to become familiar. I stood outside the fence, feeling icy cold in the hot sun and remote from my surroundings—this moment was suspended in time, it hung upon the air, motionless but quivering as a dragon-fly over still, dark water.

I think he was in there for half an hour—it seemed a lifetime. They walked about talking to Astra, and Monika showed Bill how to use the sticks as a warning or guide, to deflect the animal's head as she came close and to stroke her back as she passed.

It was fascinating, rather exhilarating, but intensely nerve-wracking. Bill had a cigarette when he came out. It is very strange to watch the person you love risk his life. After all we are not lion-trainers and we were not fooling ourselves—any time that lioness had wanted she could have dispatched us with very little trouble.

I went in after lunch. I felt very cool and very taut—stretched like an extended spring. Lions look much larger when there is no wire between you. I wonder if we look larger or smaller to them. I felt quite calm in an odd sort of way, but when I came out I was breathless and my legs were trembling. I had a cup of tea. People began to laugh and joke—tension relaxed. The first time you venture into the unknown is usually the most difficult time—you do not know what to expect, you cannot imagine what situations you may have to face. As we drove home that evening I felt utterly exhausted—drained of every feeling except a longing to hurry back to our house at Nyeri—25 miles away and to the children. To three of the people I loved most in the world, William, Louise, and Justin. Many people had seemed amazed that we should decide to take our children with us on this adventure—stories of troubles in Kenya alarmed them, and they worried over problems of food and water, insects and wild animals. I must admit we did not share their doubts. The children are part of us and part of our lives and there-fore part of our joys and our sorrows, our comfort, our pain and wouldn't we have been selfish to deny them this wonderful ex-perience? We had two people to care for them—our dear Nanny, who had been with us for three years, and was part of the family, and a young governess who was to teach the eldest their lessons and help to explore the new world of the African bush, its birds, insects and animals. We carry our own world with us, our reality and our strength, and this way we hope we never lose sight

*Sticks as a warning*

of the true values of life. The world of films is a world of make-believe—inconstant, insecure and often frightening, and all too many people are driftwood, floating inevitably towards loneliness and death, afraid and forgotten.

Oh, the joy of the smiling faces of the children, the excited voices, the log fire burning in the open hearth—home. Whatever happens, these things are what matter in life.

A pattern developed over the next five weeks. Every morning very early, we left home—leaving behind us the low grey clouds that envelop Nyeri and its dripping coffee plantations in the early morning. As we climbed higher towards the plains of Naro Moru we broke through this enveloping curtain into the early sunshine. Light slowly streaked across the horizon, throwing golden paths across the fields of pale, golden cream tall grass. This is a cultivated part of Kenya, reasonably populated; but even here it is not too hard to imagine those days 100 years ago, when each hill concealed a danger, and each step was a step into the unknown. The violet mountains rise in marvellous shapes into the distance—here and there a brightly coloured bird flew up in our path or a flock of quail rose startled from a dry gorse bush. Dust road, red dust, low bush—a lonely jackal slinking away, furtive and secret—and above us all the Kenya skies—heavy with rolling banks of fleecy clouds, their whiteness deepening to violet, purple and black. For some reason or other these clouds hardly ever obscure the sun—and for me, they are one of the finest beauties of this country.

We trained each morning with the circus lions—trying to establish more and more contact. It was not easy. Whatever points had been argued in favour of using circus animals were becoming outweighed by points in their disfavour. Let us be clear on this—it was not the fault of the lions. But they are not domestic animals. They are trained to obey commands with the whip or the sticks and it is highly improbable that in a few weeks—or even months—we could undo the training of seven and ten years respectively. When they come to you they do not come to receive affection, nor to give it— they come for a reward, for meat. Nor are they predictable—as was proved on more than one occasion. I remember very clearly a morning towards the end of June. Bill and Monika entered the cage to train with Astra—she crouched forward, her ears back and when she advanced towards them it was not to play—another element was involved. She circled round them, determined to get at Bill, her large yellow eyes hard and bright. I watched frozen and helpless outside the cage—praying 'Oh, my God, don't let anything happen.' Monika fended Astra off with her sticks—both she and Bill had become deathly white—and at last Bill managed to leave the cage. No one said very much, no one needed to. The following day Astra behaved in a similarly aggressive way towards George Adamson, myself and Bill for the second time. This time the training had been witnessed by the director and he immediately withdrew Astra from training.

Who can say what causes a lion or lioness to have a personality change? A strange smell on the wind? The sharp sour smell of our fear, which we try so hard to conceal? The smell of other lions lingering on our clothing, although we washed and changed completely when transferring from one set of lions to the other? All was not well, nerves were on edge. We were losing ground.

*They come for a reward*

About a week after we had entered the lion's cage we had two new arrivals to the camp. Boy and Girl. They were a young lion and lioness of about nine-and-a-half months—weighing approximately 130 lbs.—who had been mascots of the Scots Guards based in Nairobi and had been cared for since their discovery at about ten days old by Sergeant Ryves, their devoted friend and guardian, who now brought them to Naro Moru. Our producers had heard about these lions just as they were to be flown to England, as the regiment was shortly to leave Kenya, and they had been given permission to use them in the film. Boy and Girl. Little did we know, when we introduced ourselves to them, what a large part they were to play in our lives and how much we were to grow to love them.

We had never had friends like this before: so tremendously affectionate, such dynamic personalities, whose sudden fast movements and lightning awareness kept you constantly alert, and whose great potential commanded your respect. Of course there were some alarming moments for us, that was only to be expected, but on the whole we were increasingly astonished by what we were able to do together. George watched us with an approving smile, an occasional boyish chuckle which gave us great confidence. He seldom said anything except a bit of information which he felt we needed to know, from his own experience. I think he wanted us to find out for ourselves—to absorb our mistakes and falls early on, like a child learning to walk. He would often join in with us and his kind gentle attitude towards the lions became the stamp of our own behaviour towards them. No attempt at domination—George was as kind and considerate, open and goodnatured with them as he was with his human friends.

Our days were full. Other animals arrived from the Nairobi Orphanage—a lion called Ugas, a fourteen-month-old lioness called Mara, two cheetahs and three tiny cubs—little Elsa, Spotty, and Big Boy. Mara was an unknown quantity to us—we knew she had been a personal pet until eight months old and then given to the Orphanage, but we did not know of her great capacity for loving. Certainly, when we first went into the cage with her on her arrival, she was tremendously affectionate, hugging us, licking us, and obviously enjoying our company. She also happened to enjoy woollen jerseys, as when I glanced down after a particularly en-thusiastic embrace, I noticed that an enormous hole had appeared in the front of my cardigan—and Mara was licking her lips apprecia-tively! The three cubs were adorable—five weeks old, soft, furry and vulnerable—but already armed with needle-like teeth and tiny claws as I discovered all too soon! Little Elsa was smaller than her brothers and won my heart—we had a lot of scenes together in the film and I already felt a very special affection for her. Funny moments, exciting, thrilling, joyful and frightening moments—the days flew by and the time when we were to begin filming loomed dismayingly near.

We had always known that we would be faced with many unusual and difficult problems during the making of this film, but we had not been prepared at all for the critical one that now hung over us each minute of our waking hours. The producers had cast a circus lioness as Elsa, and we knew in our hearts that if there was the slightest chance that we were going to be able to do the things in the film script—written in London before the author had even visited Naro Moru or seen any of the lions—then we would have to do them with the Kenya lions with whom we were already estab-lishing a similar kind of relationship to that of the Adamsons and Elsa—a relationship based on mutual trust, friendship and love. Could a circus animal incensed with the indignities it had suffered for years look at us with eyes of trust and love? Would it ever be possible to convince the audience that the sullen tolerance and apathy with which the lions regarded us were really feelings of warmth and affection? Could even the most experienced actor conceal his own feelings of fear and apprehension under these circumstances? How could close contact scenes be played between the actors and the animals when the actors could not take their eyes off the animals for a moment, and the animals were only waiting for the actor to come off guard? Was this the way to tell *Born Free*? Our position was very difficult and somewhat delicate. We had asked, in our contracts, that no doubles should be used without our consent, believing that as far as our relationship with the lions was concerned, only the truth would be adequate for this unique story.

There would no doubt be enough hazards even in working with the Kenya lions, but we felt that if we suffered injury from them, less controlled though they were, it would somehow be unintentional, and at least we had a working partnership going between us. The hazards with the circus lions already seemed insurmountable. The producers, unfortunately, seemed unwilling to see our point of view—perhaps because, for some reason best known to themselves, they rarely watched the training, and therefore did not know what we were unable to do with the circus animals, and what we were increasingly able to do with the Kenya lions—notably Boy and Girl, and to a lesser extent at this stage, Mara. Their decision to use the circus animals was no doubt supported by two major considerations which were understandably important to them. They had spent a lot of money on them already—bringing them and their trainer and assistant from Europe; and they felt too, that with these lions they could roughly estimate a budget. In one form or another, using trick camera shots, a film could somehow be completed.

We began the film with the circus lions. The early scenes did not involve us to any great extent, although Bill had a scene to do walking out on the plains with Astra. Fortunately the occasion turned out to be rather comical, for as he walked behind her, the sound of his boots swishing in the tall dry grass, the tall grass which was so strange to her and by which she was pathetically bewildered, gave her a terrible fright and she took to her heels. She could just as easily have turned on him in her fear and struck.

After a few weeks of filming, which had produced little of value and had been slow and difficult, it became apparent to the producers and director that if the film was indeed going to be made they would have to use the Kenya lions. The circus lions were virtually dropped. Elsa was re-cast.

We were openly delighted, as was George Adamson and various other people who agreed that this story was impossible to make with circus animals. But combined with our happiness was the knowledge that the onus of responsibility now fell upon us. We had pleaded the case of the Kenya lions and now it was up to us to make things work. We knew only too well that there were various members of the film company all too eager to seize on our mistakes and our failures and to prove we had been wrong. People who believed almost to the end, no doubt sincerely, that the circus lions should have been used. We realized that this element existed, and whereas it was deeply discouraging and often difficult to understand, perhaps it became an added incentive to us and made us push ourselves to the limits of our resources, both mental and physical. We had so much to learn—so many unknown paths to explore, and the time now allotted to us was so little—but so precious—moments as scattered as the tall cream lilies, waving solitarily on the plains, treasured but few.

The walks with George and the lions in the dew-fresh mornings, the moments of quiet communication and rest under the thorn trees, while the bright midday sun cast sharp black shadows on to the now dry and dusty earth and all sensible lions and people seek refuge from its fierce rays. The lunchtime picnics together in the heart of the bush, picnics sometimes shared by the lions in the literal sense of the word, for although they usually wrinkled up their noses in disgust when offered a piece of ham or chicken, one young lioness, Henrietta, from the Uganda Orphanage, had a passion for a variety of items from our table—including hard-boiled eggs, tinned cream and sardines! Dear, funny Henrietta.

The months of filming and training stretched endlessly before us —what would they bring—excitement, danger, satisfaction, or failure? One thing was certain, that in spite of the great demands made upon us by the filming schedule alone, we had to try never to lose our contact with the lions—nor our understanding; but we must now assay to apply what we had learned and what we still learned every day to making a film—a film, which without this contact and understanding could never be made.

# PHOTOGRAPHS AND TEXT

*by*

*Bill Travers*

'*All animals are equal, but some animals are more equal than others.*'

George Orwell

While Ginny and I were making the final preparations to leave England for Kenya with the children, a single remark, made with great conviction at a chance meeting, was to direct much of our energy and time on a course we might never, otherwise, have seriously considered.

'I'm sure you ought to keep a record of your adventures in Africa; if you do, however inadequate it may be, it will always mean a great deal to you both.'

We met Ronald Politzer at Lambeth Town Hall at a Commemoration Service for Violette Szabo, a British agent shot during the war, whose tragically short life Ginny had portrayed in a film. He had an arresting quality in his deep voice, and his enthusiasm for the film, and all we were hoping to do, almost rivalled our own. He obviously made a great impression on us, for a few days later Ginny bought the largest diary obtainable and I bought a rather expensive camera.

It is very sad that Ronald died during the making of the film for I always intended that he should see the inadequate results of his suggestion and know the truth of his statement.

To keep a record did not on the face of it seem a very big undertaking. We started the moment we sailed from London docks and kept a sort of ship's log for practice which seemed fairly easy and was in fact rather enjoyable. The children were our subjects and we had plenty of time. But when we got to Kenya and became involved in training we encountered many problems. I was still unfamiliar with such a complicated piece of machinery as the camera, and I found it difficult to work with the cumbersome equipment dangling about my neck. I was so absorbed watching and working with the lions that I seldom remembered that I wanted to record the action, until it was all over. Ginny was so exhausted after a long day's training that when we got home she could hardly keep her eyes open long enough to write down everything. This was all such a new experience for both of us and so many things happened so quickly; it was very frustrating.

What was especially disappointing was that although I used my camera many times in the short period of training with the circus lions, the results never captured a natural relationship or sense of freedom which we knew must exist if we were to tell the story on celluloid. These circus lions lived in compounds which were no better than very large cages and they were never taken outside except to drive around camp in our caged Landrovers to get accustomed to being transported. It was impossible to photograph without getting a background of wire and supports and occasionally of someone sitting outside with a gun ready in case anything went wrong. Not to include these in the photographs was, I felt, somehow cheating, as it did not present the true facts.

Inside the compound we felt as much prisoners as the lions did and we began to resent the people who stood outside. Except for a few moments when these large circus lions lay down, tired and bored, we could not sit down near them. They invariably looked sullen and resentful, and it seemed that nearly all my photographs recorded these expressions. I sincerely feel they were disgusted with the whole human race, and they had my sympathy.

Ginny kept her diary; but I knew from her unhappiness and resentment at the conditions of life which had existed for these once noble creatures, that she was having the same problems as I. Neither of us could see how a film could be made about love, happiness, natural affection and trust between a lioness and two human beings unless such a relationship were created. We now believed from our observations that the producers and director were on the wrong track and we said so. Perhaps our recording of events to that point had a value, even if it was a very negative one. In fact until a few weeks later, when the circus lions were replaced by natural or Kenya lions, we rather doubted whether a film of *Born Free* could be made at all.

However, if I had thought it would be easier to photograph these natural lions in the delight of freedom on the open plains, I was completely mistaken. They moved so fast and so freely that they were either too far away or halfway down the lens hood. They would invariably include me in the rough play just as I was about to click, which more often than not resulted in a heavy camera impression down the front of my face and, once, some loose teeth. But the reward could be tremendous. To see these beautiful creatures with their bursts of speed, tearing through the grass, made one's blood surge; and when one was lucky enough to capture these moments, the days which followed were filled with excitement waiting for the developed film to be returned. What was more important, a sense of genuine affection and trust between the lions and us began to show. I no longer worried about taking good photographs; I tried only to record the feeling of the moment.

Boy and Girl, brother and sister, born Kenya, 1963, were our first free lions. They played so beautifully together, and no matter how long I now spent watching them I always longed to be able to look again at their graceful, rhythmic lines and their keen eyes watching each other as they traced curving patterns through sun-scorched grass.

The early sun softens the morning's edge, Girl and Ginny wander
through the whistling thorns which hum in the gentle breeze, as a continuo
for the bright, clear melodies of birds. Who could have foretold this
curious companionship which started, as perhaps all real friendships
should, with the simple things.

These two, who only a few weeks ago were more strange to each other than strangers, appreciate now the wealth of the natural setting, and in doing so learn how to spend time together comfortably. Occasionally they are arrested by an unfamiliar, eye-catching object. Ginny watches carefully to understand Girl's reaction.

The Weaver birds' abandoned nests are regarded with curiosity and a certain mistrust. The time to give her an encouraging pat or not? To know what to do and what not to do, and when not to do it, is indispensable knowledge to be found in no textbook on lions. We resorted to trial and error, but the error could be costly; a lioness this size is fully equipped to kill.

Some moments were completely unforeseen . . . a persuasive call severing too quickly the reflective mood.

The thought interrupted . . . the unexpected response. A desire to play? Eyes that failed for a moment to recognize, perhaps?

A few seconds are dilated into the endlessness of a bad dream. Correct reaction is contrary to natural instinct: lack of movement; soft voice talking; kind, if dry-mouthed, words; the gradual unfolding of the embrace and recovery of composure. A friendly pat and the walk continued.

Was it in fun? Her game? If so, we didn't know the rules yet.

Our game was football. Even a lion knows the basic rules. The simple conflict for possession.

The predator's keen eyes, that follow so easily anything in flight.

Girl; lean, lithe, leaping.

Boy stretching

Both tumbling

. . . until the ball is trapped and still.

The state of marvellously pleasurable, pointless exhaustion is reached, surveyed with satisfaction by George, the benevolent games master and occasional referee.

We were delighted to find they enjoyed football so much; it was an easy way to take the bounce out of them. After a few games, however, they turned the tables by discovering how to take the bounce out of the ball, and 'new ball' was demanded with alarming regularity. Fresh consignments were hurried from Nairobi, where it was thought we had all gone football-crazy.

George Adamson loves lions.

The trust and the tranquillity of two companions, perceptive predators, for whom the bush is always alive with incident, for whom a cloud's shadow creeping across the yellow mist of saffron-dusted fields, swallowing the dark pond-green acropanthera bush, will always be a fascination.

Boy, majestic on the earth below, serenely scans the shifting scene. Unemotional, elegant: contentedly lazing. One talks about the dignity of animals and the dignity of man.

'Trees where you sit shall crowd into a shade,' says Pope.

'Their strength is to sit still,' saith Isaiah. 'Exactly what I was trying to do,' said George.

One hears so much about twisting the lion's tail these days. Thank goodness they had a few undignified moments among themselves.

The producer's schedule presented us with a problem. We were obliged to film six normal working days a week, but before filming began each day we needed a couple of hours to establish good contact with the lion with which we would be working. If we left very early in the morning and the unit set up without us, we were able to gain this precious time. But it wasn't as simple as that. We often worked with two or more lions in one day. Furthermore those lions we did not use at all that day had to be exercised, and contact still had to be maintained with them. We could not hope to play a scene with a lion that had been brought straight on to the set from its compound. It would be much too playful and full of bounce. We could only afford to turn our backs on the lions when they had accepted our being there and were in a fairly good frame of mind; and then it did not always work. To complicate matters there were also new arrivals. We had scenes to play with some of these and now we had no time left to establish any sort of contact with them. There are no long summer evenings on the equator, only our lunch hour remained, which we were reluctant, with such exhausting work, to sacrifice.

But safety, we knew, depended a lot on preserving our friendship and on meeting newcomers under happy conditions for both parties. After all, they were as suspicious of us at first as we were of them, though we tried not to show it. So lunch-boxes were made up and whenever we could we had, with one lion or another, a picnic—of sorts.

Mara, two years old, believed that George was her mother. When it came to mealtimes she pacified herself with a shirt-sucking session. There was little George could do except chuckle weakly, 'Mara, don't be such a lunatic,' and other equally crushing rebukes. There was little we could do except laugh rather unsympathetically and to be thankful we did not affect her the same way, and to wait while she relished her imaginary meal.

On damp days we had our meals in the back of the Landrover in which the lions travelled. Mara usually wandered round the bushes until we had finished eating, but on occasions she would climb up on to the roof and take swipes at us with her huge paws as we went for second helpings.

Although she was very playful at mealtimes we were unable to persuade her to accept any of the delicious titbits we held under her nose. In fact she would just sniff them and pull an excruciated face and show her teeth as if she were absolutely disgusted with our diet.

A tea break back at camp provided her with the opportunity for further fun and games; and yet if she behaved well it worried us.

One day, as we were getting ready to film, she sat outside the tent without moving for half an hour or more, completely ignoring us. Ginny became quite alarmed and asked me if I thought that we had offended her in some way, or even more alarmingly suggested she was ill. As I looked at her more I did think she looked a little unwell, so I moved closer.

As I studied her I could feel my forearms prickle. Her ears moved back, her brow crumpled and her eyes were all bright, dancing with challenge and laughter. It was just her super naughty look.

Fortunately I had left my camera with Robin, one of the caged camera crew.

The real life events within the camp were often more dramatic than those we were trying to create on film.

One of the circus lions, Dschuba, rather elderly and unpredictable, with whom we had worked a good deal when we first arrived, had become very temperamental. It happened about the time we were discussing whether the film should, or could not, be made with circus lions. I do not believe she was worried at the thought of her part being played by another actress. Her lack of interest at 'rehearsal' showed she wasn't really ambitious in that direction. It seemed as if she had decided to follow her true feelings and from her circus training had a genuine disaffection for people, which from time to time asserted itself. Indeed so much so, it became necessary to separate her completely and to blanket her off by attaching reed matting screens round part of her compound to prevent her rushing at the wire—a tactic we felt sure might easily cause a heart attack to the unsuspecting passer-by.

Then it was thought she might be pregnant. No one knew for certain that she had not been accidentally mated before she had been acquired by the film company. There was a good deal of speculation in the camp, but Ginny felt sure from her attitude she was about to produce cubs, although really there were no visible signs. Ginny having had three 'cubs' herself was quite an authority on the subject. Eventually Dschuba hid herself in her own small darkened room and everyone was pretty convinced. At about ten o'clock on Saturday morning, 11 July, Dschuba started to bring the first cub into the world. I had called to see her and was about to leave. I felt sure she would resent my presence, but, on the contrary, she seemed to welcome it, and appeared reassured when I talked to her. For me, to be present at the time of, or to witness, a birth has always stimulated the religious demands of my conscience and coloured my appreciation of the everyday happenings of life. I am profoundly moved by birth and death.

She parted the cord well enough but the cub was tragically blue and naked, immature and stillborn. Pathetically she tried to lick it back to life. The second arrived thirty minutes later. It was very small.

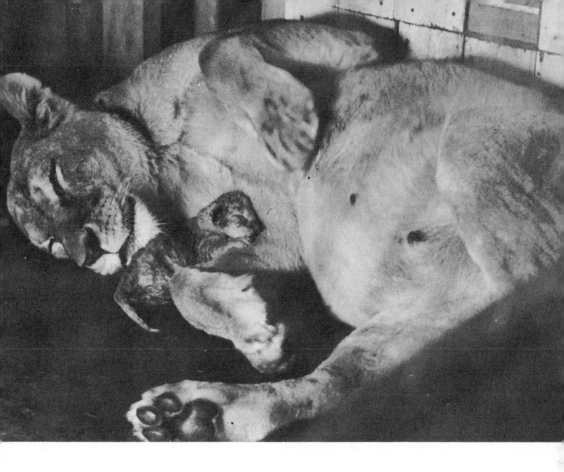

She lay back exhausted as the tiny wet, furry kitten cried and tried to move its feeble limbs.

There was an interval and then the third and fourth arrived, both equally delicate, though the last one bellowed lustily.

But it was only in the firstborn that she was interested; the one that wouldn't move.

We became very worried when she continued to ignore her three babies who were now frantically crying for attention. We felt, as did Monika, Dschuba's trainer, that if we could somehow extricate the dead one that was causing her such distress she might concentrate on those that were alive and allow them to feed. However, this presented an almost impossible task and it was not until the following morning that Ginny was able, when Dschuba suddenly started pacing round her room, to slip her slender arm under the door—there was a small gap of two or three inches for cleaning purposes—and while we watched ready to warn her, she slowly pulled out the little lifeless body. Although this had the desired effect, and Dschuba did allow the three other cubs to feed a little they became weaker and weaker. The local veterinary officer arrived. He said he knew nothing about lions but thought if we took them away from her so soon after birth they would die. That night we installed heaters all round the room to try to make a sort of incubator, hoping somehow to get them over the first few critical days.

But the next morning they were all dead.

Ginny was very upset and could hardly work with the other lions that day.

We buried them by the river bank. Nuru borrowed George's shovel and dug a grave and as I put the soft little velvet bodies into it, he looked at me with a sad, wistful smile and I could see his dark brown eyes were brimming with tears.

Perhaps nothing we could have done would have saved them. Perhaps they were too small and weak to survive, but in my quiet moments I don't always believe this. Although we have never discussed it, I don't think Ginny does either.

In fairness to Dschuba, there had been one other time when she had accepted us in a most heartening manner.

It happened a few weeks before she gave birth. She was not resentful of our being with her and she did nothing when I sat on the ground in front of her to take photographs. However from the time she lost her cubs, her personality changed and she became positively dangerous. Not only did we lose our contact with her, but up to the end of the film no one was able completely to trust her again.

It was sad. But although contact had been lost with her it was blossoming with the other, non-circus, Kenya lions, much more wild yet much more naturally affectionate.

Ginny was finding new playmates of all ages. Some irresistible newcomers had just arrived from the Nairobi Orphanage. Spotty, Big Boy, and of course, Little Elsa.

The original Elsa had been nannied by Pati, the Adamson's pet hyrax. Now we had two of them; one to play the important role of Pati and the other her stand-in. They adored to sit on Ginny's shoulder and mutter in her ear. It always sounded as if they were saying 'Tut-tut' about the world, but I cannot believe that this was true as they were very sweet and happy, and interested in everything, especially creamy rose petals, which they ate with relish.

Unlike the original Pati, they weren't very fond of lions. They would just about tolerate 'Little Elsa' and she was always a bit doubtful about them, for that matter.

Each week more lions arrived. In fact the place was becoming littered with lions.

Making contact with one of the new arrivals produced wonderfully tender, blissful moments.

There were also moments not to be shared by any but the lions themselves; proud, a pride, seemingly free; yet bound by the stringent rules and regulations of a society created for survival.

The tender caress of that big rough rasping, skin-removing tongue.

The tongue.

And the teeth . . . Ugas, a magnificent male playing with Millie from Switzerland who came to Naro Moru to 'lend a hand' for a short time. Lions show affection with their mouths.

Too much affection all at once; big loving teddy-bear hug; claws well retracted; some 300 lbs. of over-demonstration. There is no intent to harm, but when a cat is playing with a mouse it all looks harmless enough —at one stage.

Ugas loved everyone too much.

To prepare for the various scenes we tried to acquaint our lions with some of the strange objects they would be seeing in the course of filming. We had tables and tents and chairs etc., but the company couldn't risk a real camera and so supplied us with their version of it: a paraffin tin and bits of wood.

The fascination of a shining metal surface; the innocent curiosity of children; the mistrust of the mother.

I personally believe all they thought was that we had fixed an awful old paraffin tin on some bits of wood to see what they would do—probably because we'd been out in the sun too much! In any case it really was pretty obvious that the cameras would have to be caged, if only for the operators' sake—and so, for that matter, would the director and the crew!

. . . or there well might be a situation like this!

An audience accentuated Mara's sense of humour and fun—a lovely actress, she was a great player to the gallery, sometimes at our expense.

One incident in the film required a lioness on the lower limb of a tree some 12 feet above the ground. For some weeks George and I had been getting her used to climbing various trees out on the plains. At last we felt that she would do it. But when the cameras were ready it was George who was climbing about the branches; she had very cleverly got him into just the right position.

However, once Mara had made her point she co-operated several times quite happily and the director was delighted.

Whatever the difficulties, the experimental nature of our work was always stimulating. One day we had a very simple little scene to play. All that the director required was for Girl to be sitting in the grass next to Ginny's chair while Ginny was painting a landscape; I was to walk casually up to the two of them, talk to Ginny and then wander off. We tried for hours and hours which started to run into days and days.

She would either face the wrong way with her backside to the camera, or get up to greet me as I arrived, or attempt to join in the dialogue halfway through the scene, or steal the chair or paints. We tried so many times that she got bored and eventually wouldn't sit near Ginny's chair. We decided we needed some strong attraction to hold her attention.

We put a chicken in a stout cage with a loudspeaker tied on top, through which we could play very loud pre-recorded chicken noises. This cage could be hauled up by means of a rope thrown over a high bough. Our plan was that when Girl passed the spot where we wanted her to sit, the sound man would turn up the recording. It worked. Girl stopped and was amazed to see and hear such an articulate chicken up a tree. She sat down to watch and the moment she got tired of gazing up we cut off the sound and started to play the scene. How could we have been so misguided as to think she would stay there?

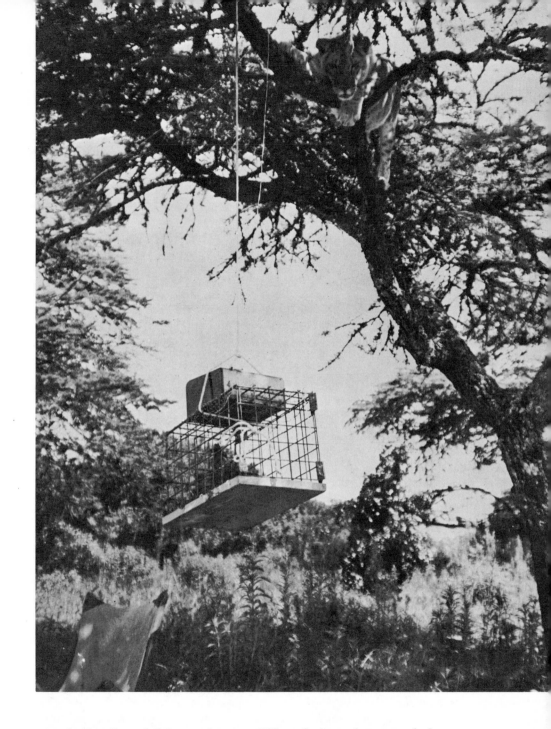

On the first line of dialogue she was off like a flash up the tree and after the chicken. The director frantically ordered the chicken to be lowered to safety.

As soon as she saw the chicken descending she slithered almost head first down the tree to catch it on the ground. As she came down so it went up. The chicken was soon going up and down like a department store elevator in an early silent comedy film. Girl was thoroughly enjoying the game of course. She never allowed us time to rescue the bird when it was in the down position, so we just had to keep going until she eventually gave up.

But the game taken to its logical conclusion provided the answer. Eventually, when the chicken had been rescued and taken away, quite of her own accord, Girl sat exhausted and, as it happened, in exactly the right spot.

So peaceful by the river bank. From their positions of safety the cameras and crew are poised ready to record the scene. The director has the word 'Action' hovering in his breath, but Girl, bored with watching the completely bewildering antics of people in cages, has already decided that something which caught her eye earlier, should be examined more closely.

The white soft, round cushion needed to be played with, bitten and chewed. Even though the taste was disgusting.

And no persuasion of Ginny's could make her give up her new best toy. As I stood and watched Ginny laughing and chasing Girl, the background of conflicting advice on what to do seemed a strangely unsympathetic chorus, though I am sure it was not intended.

I knew the tremendous effort that she was making to repair the damage, both mental and physical done several weeks before on Tuesday, 14 July —in fact only a few days after the death of the little cubs.

The circumstances and the near tragedy of that day will, I am sure, remain savagely mirrored in my mind as long as I live.

We had set out late that afternoon, about 3.30, with Boy and Girl for the airstrip training area; a place we used a good deal during those early days, because there were few trees or bushes, except around the edge, and we could see the lions more easily and so had more control if they wandered off.

We decided not to remove their leather harness and leads that day, I remember, because it was rather late and it always took a while to get them on again, if they hadn't had enough exercise and did not wish to go home. This decision was to play an important part in what subsequently happened.

As we let them out of the Landrover we realized they were very excited about something. They had seen what we had failed to see and set off at speed to shorten the distance—Boy with less deadly intent, trying to trip and tumble Girl. She had more singleness of purpose.

The Thompson's Gazelles, startled for a moment, stood to watch the old Landrover disgorge its unfamiliar contents. Their tails nervously twitched, erratically wagged from side to side, oddly giving the impression of welcome and great happiness at seeing the lions. But this was far from their real feeling. The stalk began. From seemingly harmless beginnings sometimes stem the saddest endings.

Boy and Girl gained fifty yards, moving only when the gazelles had arched their slim graceful necks and dipped their heads to nibble the grass, freezing in their tracks if one suddenly looked up. The gazelles were indiscernibly, but definitely, aware of them, and casually wandered further away by precisely another fifty yards. And so the distance, too great for a final rush attack, was inconspicuously maintained.

But the lions could not understand why we did not join them. Little bites, persistent pushing with paws, great agitation and low miaowing. At first we did not realize what they wanted us to do, but the moment we crawled forward with them, that all stopped. Flattered by the privilege of being part of a pride we imitated their movements. It was a game, their game, now.

Half an hour later there was no significant change in the relative distances between our party and the gazelles and these young inexperienced lions grew bored. As Ginny straightened up and turned to me, Boy seizing the opportunity, leapt. They both went crashing to the ground. I heard a crack like a dry stick breaking.

We four alone, on the gentle folds of that field. Ginny lay on the ground moaning softly, prone and vulnerable.

'My leg is broken.'

'I know.'

The lions perhaps thought it was part of the game.

How quick the mind can change from one absorbing interest to another.

I ran and with more strength than I possess, but which is given on occasions like this, I dragged the lions by their leather harness a few yards away.

I desperately needed something to distract them from what could be an extremely dangerous situation. In the cold, clammy second which followed, I suddenly remembered that only two days before I had enticed them out of a bush by flapping my shirt. I tore it off and, as controlled as possible, began to drag it over the little hummocks of grass.

They looked and, for one endless, suspended heartbeat, they paused and so, I felt, did my life. Then they raced towards me.

We stopped only at the Landrover, into the back of which I threw my now tattered shirt. Boy followed and I slid shut the tail gate. Girl climbed on the roof. I could not risk opening the back again, but somehow I felt she would stay there.

Not daring to run, I returned to gather Ginny in my arms, watched by Girl, who was now content to sit on the roof and observe. I placed Ginny, as tenderly as I could on the front seat.

I then persuaded Girl, with a few scrapings of bone marrow left over from the 'treats' which I noticed on the floor of the Landrover, to join Boy in the back. Slowly we set off along the rutted cotton soil track, some four miles back to camp.

Very late that night we arrived at Nairobi. The 126 miles had been a nightmare drive in the back of a Fiat Estate car. The doctors, anaesthetist and nurses bustled along the hollow corridors.

As I sat in that bleached hospital room the next day Ginny smiled sadly through the anaesthetic's clouding effect. I knew she was already hazily wondering what she would be wondering for many weeks to come—how to start again the work that had only just begun; to go back and show no sign of fear; to do nothing that would betray the existence of a nervous heart, either to the human-beings around the camp, who might perhaps be fooled, or much more significantly, to the lions.

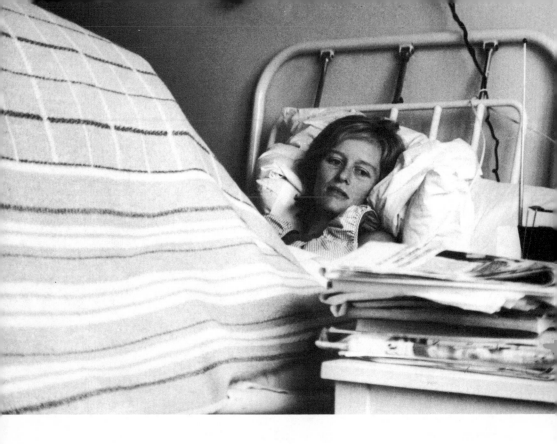

In hospital, awaiting that unpredictable moment, was perhaps a sort of purgatory for Ginny. There was little I could say to alleviate the agony in her mind. I had not yet told the children who were waiting at home. William, aged five, Louise, aged three and Justin, eighteen months.

During the next few weeks I made many trips to Nairobi, driving fast at dusk, through the villages and settlements which blinked like fireflies in the greedy darkness.

Ginny had five general anaesthetics; the bones were set and re-set and a steel screw was used to ensure union and greater accuracy. Plaster casts were changed and stitches removed. All the care and ingenuity of a very fine orthopaedic surgeon was employed. But Ginny was pale and troubled beneath her warm smile of welcome. She talked of the children a great deal and I knew how much she missed them; and then of almost anything, the camp, the lions, holidays we had spent together on Elba, but all vaguely as if it existed a few thousand light years away. I realized how great the shock had been and how much damage had been done to her confidence in those few moments. She knew that the longer she lay in bed, the more difficult would become the task, both mentally and physically. Any minor setback in her recovery immediately became a catastrophe. The whole business had in fact assumed different proportions; it was no longer just a job, a film, a part to be played; it had become a challenge, a Matterhorn, to be climbed and sometimes, no doubt, during those long hospital nights, an Everest.

Somehow your whole perspective is changed when you are playing with lions.

It was very difficult to leave Ginny when she was so vulnerable to her thoughts. The actor's imagination is of necessity an over-developed one, and is not always an asset. Even for me at that time, I only had to look at the script for the whole thing to seem completely impossible.

I usually set out before dawn to drive back to camp in time for early morning training. There is some quality, some vibration in the atmosphere, which makes Kenya quite different to anywhere else. People become much more emotional, arguments much more inflamed, and causes much more desperate. As I drove along in the grey-green half light, reflected from the night cool opal sky, I knew that Ginny could never start again exactly where she left off; that somehow the lions must have more regard for her comparative frailty. They must be persuaded somehow not to stalk, jump up and knock her down; they were too powerful and unbelievably strong. But how?

We needed the lions to be wild and natural with us for the film. We needed their love and affection. Also we needed them to respect our inferior strength. We as animals had asserted ourselves over the rest and dominated them by using weapons. Now we were trying to share life with the next most dominating predator in the world without weapons. It was a difficult task. The margin of safety was small. George Adamson was deeply concerned when I talked to him about my thoughts and my impressions in Nairobi. He said that Elsa had, to a lesser degree, the same unfortunate habit. Both he and Joy had been waylaid a good many times, but they had never suffered more than a few large bruises. Perhaps it had been easier with only one lion. They had looked after Elsa from when she was a tiny cub and she had, of course, received more love and attention. Also they had spent so much more time with her. We could do nothing about the first two points he made, but following his line of thought, I suggested we should try to establish a better relationship with the lions and spend every available minute we could with them—even to visiting them in their compound at night. George was in complete agreement. We rearranged the compounds slightly and managed to get an old tent erected in one of them; and George went about establishing a deeper relationship in his own quiet, humorous way. He moved in to sleep at night with Boy and Girl. We reasoned too, that perhaps they stalked and jumped up on us because they got bored with just walking through the bush, or frustrated at being unable to catch gazelles. So we decided to find a more interesting training area and to invent new games. We also managed to persuade the producers to allow us a little more assistance. A very charming and fearless white hunter joined us, called Sten Cedergren.

We were determined somehow to have less 'wild' lions by the time Ginny returned.

Sten joined in enthusiastically. He was Swedish and extremely powerfully built and he soon understood the problem. With four feet off the ground, even though it was all fairly much in fun, the attack could be devastating.

We tried balloons to distract, but even then Sten was sometimes caught off guard, before he could release one.

George, the master mind solved the problem. He tied a balloon to the end of a stick and so we invented a game which the lions enjoyed.

When they had popped two or three balloons to their great satisfaction,
they became quite tired and were content to wander about with us on the
plains.

I carefully reported to Ginny in hospital any slight advance in our relationship with the lions. But I realized she was well aware that although we were making progress, as far as she was concerned there was nothing we could do to maintain the contact she had so far established; no one else could do the job for her. Perhaps this fact stimulated the stubborn fighting streak that runs through Ginny's character, for one evening I arrived and found she had mastered her crutches in half a day, and now refused to admit to any pain or discomfort whatsoever. The doctors were so impressed that she was permitted to travel back with me the following morning, on certain conditions of rest. Louise asked as she arrived, and was getting out of the car, 'Is your leg really inside that thing?' And was not satisfied until she saw Ginny's toes wiggling at the other end. The children, of course, were overjoyed to see her. We wondered what kind of welcome she would get from the lions.

It was not an easy return. The leg soon became very swollen and bulged out of the plaster. It was stiff and the crutches were cumbersome. The job was quite demanding enough when we were perfectly fit. But Ginny allowed herself only two days at home before visiting the lion camp. I knew what a strain it now was for her to wait.

I had been out on the plains with Boy and Girl and was walking them back to their compound when Ginny was driven up in our dusty Humber car. She called out to me and both lions stopped and looked round. They paused and with the second call Boy raced over and jumped up at the car door, while Girl leapt on to the roof. As Ginny opened the window a little more he pushed through his beautiful large head and greeted her, rubbing his face against her hands as if he could not understand why she had been away for such a long time. I almost called out, in case he jumped inside on top of her, but he just stood up stretching on his hind legs. I was so happy that I had not needed to interrupt the moment.

A few days later however, when Ginny went inside the compounds, it was not so encouraging. There was something false about that cold, white, plaster leg which the lions (even the cubs) could not accept—the unnaturalness that attracts, yet inhibits, children.

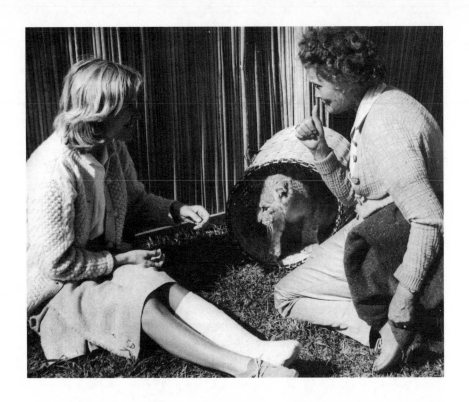

Ginny discussed this unexpected reaction with Joy Adamson, who had arrived in Kenya while Ginny was in hospital. The larger lions attacked the crutches and carried them away as if they were new toys and they backed away from the plaster with their ears well flattened. Obviously, until the artificial aids could be discarded, little could be done except sit outside the compounds and talk through the wire mesh. But it was a start and in spite of everything I felt we were back on the road again. One of the first scenes to be scheduled as soon as Ginny's plaster could be removed was the episode when George and Joy took Elsa to the seaside, not far from the beautiful beaches at Malindi. No one knew whether or not any of our lions would go into salty water. In fact we did not even know if they would go into deep water at all. The script was very optimistic; we would film scenes of us all swimming about in the sea together.

Fortunately, not far from camp there were two large ponds and we were able to get permission to use these, and the plains around them, as a new training area. We called it 'Twin Dams' and it had many advantages over all other areas we had used so far. First of all we could try to get the lions accustomed to going into the water and so make some preparation for Malindi. Secondly it was a more interesting area, abounding in many different species of wild animals and birds, and this was ideal for our plan to reduce the amount of attention the lions paid to Ginny as we walked along beside them.

At first we did nothing to encourage them to go near the water, because we felt that they needed to get used to the Twin Dams area.

There were so many new smells and winding game tracks to be followed. Boy was particularly interested. We hoped, as most of these led through the thick thorn bushes to the water's edge, that they would follow and arrive there of their own accord. But they didn't; they preferred to go in the opposite direction, perhaps following the animals who had been drinking there earlier that morning.

As that little plan had failed, we drove them in the Landrover to the water's edge, but they took one look at it and walked briskly away.

There was something they didn't like. MUD.

As soon as their feet sank a little in the soft sticky mud they snarled and wandered off. Girl seemed a little less disturbed by this unpleasant sensation than Boy; so we decided to concentrate on her.

Ginny was now able to join us for a short while each day. An enormous safari boot had been specially made to fit over her plaster and her trousers had been modified with a long zip down one leg—so the lions could not see the cast. She and the reluctant Boy watched our attempts to persuade Girl to enter the water with great interest.

We weren't making much progress when George suddenly started to chuckle and produced a balloon. Girl couldn't resist that and after a few mumbled protests she followed as it drifted across the water.

Once she was in the water, she didn't seem to mind the mud bottom at all.

Boy, much heartened by his sister's courage, came bounding down to the water's edge when she tried to land a stick, but was very careful not to get his feet wet.

Eventually Boy was persuaded to go into the water too, but not at Twin Dams. He paddled in a little freshet some distance away. I don't think he enjoyed it at all. We felt so sorry for him; he looked so miserable.

He was delighted to find an excuse to get out and chase Girl round and round the Landrover, which I'm sure was much more his idea of a boy's game. 'When youth and pleasure meet, to chase the glowing hours with flying feet.'

We sat outside George's tent that night, weighing the fortunes of the day. We believed that Girl would possibly go into the sea, but we wondered how long it would take us to persuade her to accept her new environment. The weather would be very much warmer when we dropped from 6,000 feet to sea-level. The water would be salty. There were many other factors too. Ginny's plaster had been removed but her leg was weak and soon became very swollen, and the programme of work to be done was ambitious to say the least.

We left for Malindi ahead of the main unit so that we could train on the beach, for one long weekend, before we started filming. We were optimistic in spite of the problems, perhaps because we were going to Malindi and had been told so much about the beautiful beaches. Perhaps we were fascinated by the thought of the next phase in what had now become for us an almost unbelievable adventure.

Palm trees and the whispered song of the sea. Strange sand and strange salt water and 'the little dulling edge of foam that browns and dwindles as the wave goes home'.

The smooth beach surprised by unusual footprints. The shore, of necessity deserted. Boats swinging idly in the slack, for no fishermen were there. Sea spiders and the leathery line of slippery seawrack curling carelessly along the sabulous shore.

The waves were highly suspect with their habit of disappearing and Girl was very unhappy.

I was just about to take another photograph when she took off, suddenly deciding the whole thing was too much—she nearly took Ginny with her.

But gradually we persuaded Girl to go in, and she found that, except for the salty taste, she liked it.

In practically no time she was swimming and enjoying her new game—water polo.

A nice salty, shiny, bluey-green parrot fish.

The fresh sweet-tasting water when we got home.

The days turned over like pages of a favourite book; we were regretful of their passing; we enjoyed them too much. Energy was easily spent and there were few moments of rest in the shade, on the stone damp coolness of the soft, moist sand. It was a dream-like existence; lion, man, sea and sand; a surrealistic way of life.

Girl would sleep—she probably enjoyed that as much as anything.

How innocently a lion can sleep—the sleep of children, untroubled. The logical conclusion to being awake.

And yet it was quite difficult to catch them actually asleep; at the slightest sound or movement they were instantly awake, staring—like lotus-eaters, trying to recall the escaping pleasures of a fading dream.

They would yawn, as if to brace their senses against reality . . .

. . . and yawn.

They yawn in such unexpected places. Halfway up a tree they would yawn.

Even

climbing

on tents

they YAWN. They are great yawners, but this drowsy inertia is deceptive.
The muscles need no priming; the spring is nearly always fully wound.

Many of the uncomfortable moments during training and filming were, however, attributable purely to lack of knowledge and understanding. One such moment occurred when we were trying to film a scene with a lioness inside a tent, in which Ginny was to 'mop my fevered brow' as I lay on a camp-bed with Girl (according to the script) sprawled out on the floor watching us. To do this one side of the tent was carefully removed and heavy wire mesh was substituted, leaving a small horizontal slit for the camera. A small cage into which Girl could be unloaded was placed outside the tent. By opening a sliding door from the outside Girl could walk into the tent where it was hoped she would eventually settle down.

Of course no one knew how long it would take her to settle in the right place. She might do it straight away or it might take half a day or more. But we were fairly confident she would do it eventually, because she had sat down in the tent with me many times previously, during training. George, Ginny and I thought that time could be saved if she had a lot of exercise in the morning and the scene was planned for the afternoon, especially if it was a warm day and she were well fed beforehand. Lions become very active and jumpy if the weather is cold or rainy, we noticed.

The producers had shown quite a lot of patience, but they were finding that their patience was straining their budget and vice-versa. They therefore arranged for a vet to give the lion a tranquillizer to make her sleepy. They reasoned, understandably, that in this way they could eliminate a lot of the preparation we had thought necessary. They could also plan the scene at an hour more compatible with their schedule. Perhaps they thought it would be safer for us, but we were rather worried.

It was true that tranquillizers properly prescribed were not considered dangerous to a healthy animal, but there was insufficient knowledge on this subject to be certain what the immediate and subsequent reactions would be. Animals of the same species often react differently to the same drug. Girl was particularly friendly towards both Ginny and me and we did not want to risk anything that might bring about a personality change or damage in any way our unusual relationship with her. Also, on principle, we had based our training on creating circumstances that would induce the lions to do what we wanted naturally. The matter was discussed at length at a production meeting and our arguments were rejected.

The next morning the cameras were ready. Ginny took up her position. I got into bed. The gate between the slip cage and the wired-in tent was withdrawn. Girl, doped with a tranquillizer, wandered through the opening. We were horrified to see she was pathetically bumping into everything. It was obvious she did not know what she was doing, nor do I think she could see properly. She lurched against the side of my bed and I could tell from her attitude she did not recognize me. I called her but she did not appear to recognize my voice either, as she clambered on the bed.

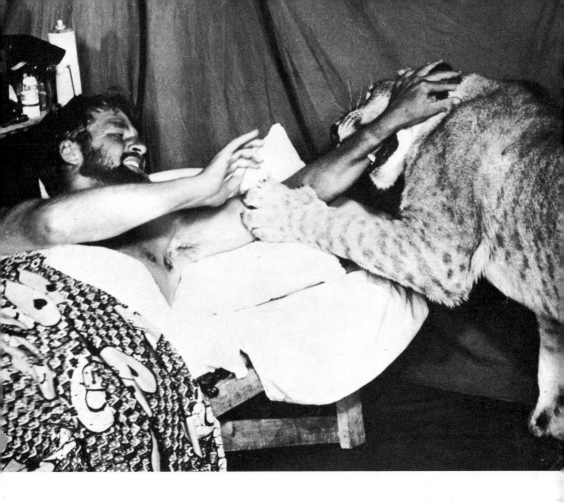

I put out my arm to fend her off but she took it in her mouth. I kept talking to her as calmly as I could, and began to think how stupid we were to put ourselves in such a position, when quite suddenly she let go of my arm, and started to miaow in a low hoarse voice. A few moments later she drunkenly staggered away.

Johnny Jay, the unit's stills photographer, took this photograph, standing outside the wire. He kindly gave me a copy as a souvenir.

We did not proceed with the scene. She wasn't her old friendly self again for several days, but then, probably, neither were we.

There is a special freedom in walking out of a tent, with the dew drying on thirst-quenched grass and scenting the morning air; the pearly canopy of smouldering cloud fanned away by the faint breeze, revealing the bluebell desert beyond; the warming, sensuous, physical touch of sunbeams. Seven miles from the Equator, 6,000 feet above the sea, all God's trees and stones are exactly as He put them there. The animals are trespassing on no one's sacred soil. The continuous moment of existence stretches on according to the greater reason we do not understand.

It is a moment of little heaven which, perhaps, birds feel as they fly from their nests, and sing about.

We were sometimes confederates, conspirators against the clock, which would call us back to begin the day's filming. We enjoyed every second of nature's harmonies.

An old worn track runs beside a tree, avoiding the sudden crumbling soil-caves of wart hogs and aardvarks, unseen in the spiny grass and perhaps unvisited. My imagination leaps a century back, as we walk along, to when the Masai, beautiful, tall, slim graceful figures of men, stood out proud upon this plain. Their mud and stick huts were grouped in the centre, where dark green blotches of matted grass now grow—like giant fairy rings in an English meadow. It is the morning when the Masai move their cattle on to new pastures and burn their huts.

How wise, for one must always move on and no one can really return. The world lives its moments and ripens along with you. I cannot make a morning mean, again, the same as this. 'Joy in looking and comprehending is nature's most beautiful gift.'

Mara walks past me as I squat. We must learn to sit as she passes and she must feel content to leave us, vulnerable, alone.

There are scenes to play sitting down, when to climb playfully over us would be quite out of place.

Ginny with my camera often achieved astonishing results. She occasionally had a slight tilt, but this usually made the picture more interesting, as happened here. Some years previously, when we were on holiday in Italy, she somehow managed to straighten up the leaning tower of Pisa, while I rocked backwards on my heels.

From almost everywhere we walked we could see Mount Kenya, pale, detached, aloof, watching, like a child's abandoned sand castle of snow, forsaken by the sea of dark green trees.

Mount Kenya was always there and we felt that she was there.

Perhaps we understood for the first time a little about mountains, as we climbed up one Sunday with the children to picnic above the 11,000 feet line, where the trees had disappeared and the rocky moorland crept up towards the snowy summits some 6,000 feet above; and what Blake meant:

> 'Great things are done when men and mountains meet;
> This is not done by jostling in the street.'

There is something too, about the stillness of a mountain when all the rest of the world, the trees, the rivers, the grass, the animals and the people are moving. From out of that stillness a little flashing trout stream hushes and murmurs as it probes through the pale blue jacaranda's tumbling flowers. It threads its way round the fringe of the garden of the old wooden settler's house we had rented. William had learned to cast and fish in it while waiting for us to come home from the lions and the day's work.

He could hardly wait to tell us of his great adventure or to show Louise his nine and a half-ouncer, caught with his 'Kenya Bug'. He thought that maybe he would just be a fisherman all his life. But at breakfast the next day he decided he didn't really like eating trout, only catching them.

The children could share no part of their lives with the lions. To the lions they were small animals to be stalked and caught. We felt from their attitude that they did not associate the children with us either by smell, shape or sound. The first visit to the compound brought the same response from all the larger lions except one and she gazed ahead, as Justin gazed ahead, with utter disregard.

The others would bound along their wire occasionally leaping up as if to climb over, or would crouch behind a tree stump ready to spring, their brown backsides twitching from side to side in nervous anticipation of what they might do were there no barrier there.

Only the very small cubs of several weeks, were friendly and safe and we brought them home on Christmas Day.

The children could not remember many Christmases before this so it did not seem so unusual to them.

A rondavel made of sticks and mud with a Chinese coolie hat of reeds on top; silver tinsel icicles in the golden equatorial sun; gem-like orbs from the settlers' stores; it seemed quite natural that the cubs would want to see the tree. The snow was on Mount Kenya.

Just two days to remember that spiritual nativity so deeply buried under two thousand years of human exploitation. The quintessence of love about which so many wars have been fought; or were they fought in the name of Christ for the actual gain of territory?

Through how many years of evolution have covetous eyes observed the ever-shrinking world—whether represented by a wasted, weedy plot beyond the farmer's fence or a weaker state beyond the royal domain? It makes no difference whether it is a patch or a kingdom; territory, not sexual desire or hunger, sparks off the fight, and lions, like other animals, fight to annex or defend the land on which they must hunt to support and establish their pride.

The clash between Elsa and another lioness, which was an important scene in the film, was induced by developing in each her sense of possession over the same piece of ground.

The unknown rocky outcrop and the suspicion that another lioness has been and may still be there. . . . Her search reveals no tenant. But still she treads warily, instinctively certain of some danger, yet with the unblissful ignorance of not knowing where the enemy is.

The touching of faces, almost a kiss, the formal, stylized greeting of deadly opponents a few seconds before their real intention becomes apparent.

The first fierce crunching collision of unbelievable strength.

Muscles knotted, bodies twisted, savage roars of anger.

A pause for breath and to re-assess the value of the land and the chances of success.

We never realized how wild and fierce our lions could be until we saw that fight. The books we had read on the voyage out and those before, like *Man Eaters of Tsavo*, had faded in our memory with our growing love and trust for our new friends, until they seemed like children's stories of fabled beasts; myths of quite another world and time. One small incident was perhaps especially responsible for this frame of mind.

One afternoon we were taking Girl out by ourselves to the plains that were our training ground, because there was no white hunter available to accompany us. At the last minute the director of publicity asked to drive out and watch from his Hillman estate car with his guest Charles McCarry of the *Saturday Evening Post*.

Girl was particularly affectionate as we trekked across the tawny suede patchwork that seemed to stretch like browning autumn into the green April forests of the Abedare foothills. She rubbed her head against our thighs and bounded off only to wait for us a few yards further on. Suddenly she stopped and sat quite still and watched. Her eyes unmoving, absorbing the whole spectacle ahead.

Twenty or thirty Thompson gazelles were flickering across the field. One could almost see her maneless nape ruffle as her head extended forward between her paws; slowly she crept forward with more purpose than I had ever seen before.

They stopped and she stopped and the stalk began. Not wishing to be involved today in this back-breaking game we wandered back to the Landrover and to where the estate car had carefully crept to a standstill. I started to explain to our guests through the window how she would gain, as she thought unnoticed, a few yards. I said how frustrating it was for her, and how at her age, according to George, she really stood no chance of catching a gazelle.

Almost as I finished speaking, fired by a burning desire to catch those provocative creatures, Girl made a lightning rush—and to our complete amazement, and that of the 'Tommies', she was amongst them. They split and she veered to the right; then suddenly she twisted round in her tracks and lashed out at one which was attempting to cross behind her. A fine young male of about five years crashed and tumbled in the grass, his back leg shattered by the blow.

By the time I had run over she was at his throat. Without ever releasing her hold she slowly rolled him over.

One step nearer and I knew that his beautiful sad eyes could no longer see and the moment of death had just then arrived.

The rest of the gazelles watched unperturbed from a hundred yards or so away; some continued grazing, some twitched their tails. They accepted his death as unemotionally as they were now accepting life.

And somehow when he died he accepted it too, without any fuss or struggle. He seemed just to wait, with his last few thoughts, for the blackness and oblivion.

Girl made no attempt to open up the stomach with her claws or to eat, but picked up her beautiful victim and carried him quite correctly between her front paws, and I walked along beside her. As she had never killed before, or been instructed by a parent, I wondered at her instinctive ability both to kill and to carry. I was more amazed by what she did next.

A yard or two in front of Ginny's feet she stopped, laid the gazelle on the ground and wandered over to greet Ginny again, as if by ritual. I could hardly believe my eyes. What bond did she feel existed between us to make such a gesture, to trust us with her kill. Were we so fortunate to be considered as part of the pride? Was she tired of carrying it, or no longer interested in it? Or did she just happen to drop it near where Ginny was standing?

We will never know for certain the answer to those questions. Nor shall we ever know what we were supposed to do at that moment. We petted her of course, and presently I helped her get the soft warm body into the back of the Landrover, where she sat holding it.

In almost stunned silence we drove back to camp.

It may well be true that situations and events are never so unusual as our imagination can make them; but then all life is only as we see it, or wish to see it.

I look back and think that perhaps we had only dreamed a long year's dream and that many of our interpretations of the wonderful moments were just wishful thinking. Perhaps we only accepted as valid—and shared —Joy's and George's attitude towards animals, and lions in particular, out of admiration for them and because we were playing their parts.

I do not think so. The validity of that attitude still seems absolute; and it will remain absolute for us, I know, for ever.

Who can forget a haunting look like this . . .

. . . or fail to remember a yesterday like this?

# Epilogue
### by
### Virginia McKenna

Where are they now, our four-legged friends, our constant companions for ten-and-a-half months—Boy, Girl, Mara, Henrietta, Ugas, Little Elsa and her brothers Spotty, Big Boy and all the rest? Are they roaming the plains in freedom fulfilling their rightful place in the world, those dignified and magnificent animals? The answer is a pitiful one. Three out of all the lions that were used in the making of *Born Free* are now with George Adamson in the Meru Game Reserve being shown the way back to a free and natural life. The three are Boy and Girl, who had been generously given to the Adamsons after the completion of the film by the Scots Guards Regiment, realizing perhaps that their much-loved lions deserved the chance to play their part in the natural cycle of life, more hazardous though it might be than a life in perpetual confinement; and after a long period of delay these two were joined by Ugas, the fully grown male from the Nairobi Orphanage.

The Adamsons, Bill and myself made unceasing but fruitless attempts to obtain as many of the lions as was possible for the purpose of rehabilitation—even for the cubs who would have been cared for until they were old enough to start on their road to freedom. Unfortunately these helpless animals were already destined to imprisonment for life—life behind bars, life in a cage, at the mercy of man's whim. As George Adamson wrote in a letter to me 'It is tragic to think that the lives of such magnificent creatures are at the mercy of people who treat them as so much merchandise, who know nothing about the feelings of animals and care less. It is the same mentality which condoned and tolerated the slave trade.'

Some of the main arguments given by the people who were opposed to the rehabilitation of the lions—and of course there were many other reasons put forward, too involved and too lengthy to discuss here—were that the animals in question were either too young or too old, and that it couldn't be done. In fact their youth was no drawback as I have already said—cubs do grow up—but it is true that certain of the lions were too old to be introduced to a new way of life, and in the case of the circus lions it would have been sheer cruelty to expect these middle-aged animals to be able to adapt themselves to freedom after their long years in captivity. Neither old lions nor circus lions were ever asked for.

To those who say that it couldn't be done I would ask—is it really that the effort to try to do it is too much? Because I can see no reason to accept this argument without allowing the attempt to be made. In any case, it has already been done successfully by the

Adamsons with Elsa and their practical experience in this field must far outweigh that of their critics. George and Joy cared deeply for the *Born Free* lions and were willing to try and make the venture work, so that these beautiful creatures should have the chance to fulfil their rightful destiny on earth.

Perhaps after all it is man who loses his dignity by his attitude towards the animal kingdom. Does it make his conscience prick less to assure himself that animals have no souls? Have we alone the right to heaven and hell?

So all we have to do now to see the *Born Free* lions is to visit them in their zoos—Paignton Zoo, Detroit Zoo, or Whipsnade, or alternatively this summer we could go to a large estate in Wiltshire where one of our peers of the realm, in conjunction with a former circus owner, is transforming part of his grounds into an English Game Reserve—for lions. He is planning to put fifty lions into an area comprising 96 acres, and is surrounding the whole with a 12-foot high fence, an electrified inner fence, and police dogs will patrol outside. On the face of it, to some people, his scheme may sound reasonable enough. The lions will live 'free'. But if what we know about lions, and all animals for that matter, fighting to establish their territory—brilliantly expounded by Robert Ardrey in *African Genesis*—might we not expect something of a bloodbath when fifty lions of different ages and from different areas are put together in such a small space? In the wild a lion's territory can range over a distance of up to 12 miles—will fifty be content to live peacefully in 96 acres? Add to this a number of well-meaning sightseers in their cars watching the endeavours of the keepers to ensure that all lions have their necessary ration of food, which is in itself an enormous task. Most casualties are caused by 'the conflict of juvenile appetites with their rigorous dominance of their elders'—to quote Mr. Ardrey. There will also be the various circus hands who are responsible for going in to remove the excrement—no sun-dry system is going to work in England—together with the qualified veterinary surgeons to attend the sick and wounded. And what about the climate—which applies to open-air zoos as well. Even with shelters, the cold, bleak, grey winter of this land is far more of a hardship than anything they would have experienced in their natural environment. Will this animal exhibition really enhance the estate at Longleat? or replenish the ancient family coffers?

I have been to Whipsnade Zoo, and I have seen Mara and Little Elsa. It was a difficult journey to make, my heart and my feet were

*Africa*

leaden for I knew no joy would come from such an expedition. Five lions were in the enclosure—four females and an enormous male. The enclosure was large—a veritable paradise compared with the London Zoo, but nevertheless a prison for our lions, who had known the miles of plain and bush of their homeland and who had chased the game through the honey-coloured grasses. Both lionesses had several rub-marks on their bodies, probably a result of their long journey from Africa, when in fear and loneliness they would have moved and pushed incessantly against the sides of their crates or cages. One of Mara's eyes looked septic (she had been involved in many fights with the male since her arrival five weeks before, the keeper told me), and the inside of Little Elsa's right front leg showed a fresh and open cut. I saw Mara first and called her—she lifted her head, her ears pricked up and she came quickly to the edge of the cage and looked at me. I started to talk to her, and she began to rub against the bars moaning and crying. I couldn't touch her—the compound was surrounded by a thick mesh fence which stood 3 feet or so outside the bars.

And then I saw Little Elsa. My very special friend with whom I had spent hours and hours quite alone in the bush, playing hide-and-seek, and running, and sitting in the shade talking—just being alive together. Moments no one had ever shared. And now I could not touch her. She heard me call, and she *ran* to the bars—she jumped up against them, crying, moaning, calling—and I so helpless and so full of love and so desperately unhappy could only call and cry too.

This—this then was the end.

George had asked for both these lionesses for his rehabilitation scheme. He had been refused. So Mara and Little Elsa (who had been parted from her two brothers) had been sent to a zoo.

What does this matter, some people will say. After all animals have not memories as we have, they do not feel similar emotions, they do not sense pain as we do, nor joy, nor sorrow, nor grief at parting from friends and companions. Can we be so sure? One particular episode during our stay in Kenya remains vividly in my mind. We had taken two lionesses to Malindi, Girl and Mara, and we were to film the beach scenes. Boy had been left behind in Naro Moru. After a few days of working with the lionesses we observed that Girl, on the one hand, was unhappy and unco-operative, while Mara, on the other hand seemed content and worked well. Was Girl pining for her brother? No one was certain, but one thing was sure—in order to film the required scenes with Girl we had to have a happy lioness. Boy was driven overnight, the 500-odd miles to the coast, and from the moment of his arrival Girl was her old self again.

As for their memories—from the time I left Kenya until the day I saw Mara and Little Elsa at Whipsnade, six months had passed—and they remembered me immediately.

How long will they remain there I wonder. For when the zoo needs re-stocking with young, virile animals, and when Mara and Little Elsa no longer serve their purpose, they will no doubt, as happens all the time, be moved on to another zoo. Will it be a first class zoo or second or even third class? Who will care about the old lionesses then—their spirits dulled and their bodies de-vitalized? Is this their reward for all the love and trust they had given to human beings?

Our hopes now are pinned on the Adamsons who, in spite of much criticism and antagonism, are training four animals to return to freedom in the Meru Game Reserve, thanks to the understanding and assistance of its Game Warden, Ted Goss. Joy is working with a young cheetah, Pippa, whom she has looked after for about a year, and although Joy has been told by experts that cheetahs cannot kill for themselves until they are two years old, Pippa often stays away from camp for as long as ten days, has been seen in the company of other cheetahs and is slowly but surely becoming more independent. The other three animals are the lions whom I have already mentioned. Before being joined by Ugas, Boy and Girl had made great strides towards their freedom. George used to take them for walks every morning, covering great distances, and stalking the many varieties of game found in the reserve. Gradually they stayed away from camp for increasing lengths of time, and soon the day came when Girl started to make her own kills. George describes two of these incidents in one of his letters.

'I was walking with Girl along the edge of the swamp, not far from camp, Boy having decided to stay at camp, when we came on a small herd of zebra. Girl made a very careful stalk to the nearest cover, a fallen tree about fifty yards away from the zebra. She sat motionless for nearly half an hour while the zebra grazed slowly towards her hiding place. When they were within fifteen yards, she made her rush and caught a large foal. She brought it down from behind and then got it by the throat and hung on. In three minutes it was dead. I was most impressed at the efficient manner in which she killed. Young lions so often make a terrible mess of killing. As usual Boy had missed the boat! I had to go and call him from camp. Unfortunately it was late in the evening so I could not take pictures.' This achievement was followed up five days later by a second when Girl, although having eaten enormously of a freshly killed water buck, disappeared again into the bush. George continues, 'in spite of being gorged with meat, Girl went off hunting during the night. Next morning there was no sign of her. I went with Boy to look for her without success. In the afternoon, my boy came to me and said that he had seen Girl sitting by the carcase of an eland. She had killed a full-grown eland! single-handed during the night! It was a remarkable effort. There had been a terrific struggle around a fallen tree. There was not a scratch on Girl.'

In spite of their increasing independence all three lions still love George and like to be in his company. He writes 'one morning, in the early hours, I woke up to find Ugas, Boy and Girl inside my tent. As there was nothing much I could do about it, I waited until they had settled down, Ugas alongside my bed, Girl at the

*Whipsnade*

head and Boy at the feet and then went back to bed to catch up on my sleep. They behaved perfectly.'

So proficient was Girl becoming at providing for herself and Boy that George no longer had to feed them. A major hurdle had been crossed. Then with the arrival of Ugas who had to be given food, the progress of the other two lions was necessarily slowed down. George could not feed Ugas and leave out the others—apart from anything else the three lions now had to get to know each other—to accept each other, and they all had to be treated on equal terms. But the groundwork is there. We know Girl could be independent and soon she will be growing up in yet another way. 'Boy and Girl are now nearly twenty-five months old', George writes, 'and I expect Girl to come into season any day. It will be interesting to see what happens. My theory is that lionesses become sexually mature earlier than lions and therefore she will not mate with Boy but with Ugas or a wild lion. It will be a difficult time for Boy but I feel sure she will come back to him after the mating period which lasts about six days.'

George's letters, read and re-read, so vividly written, so filled with concern and love for his three charges. If only he could have had more.

It would be good to sit with George and Joy outside their tent in the evening, as we used to do many months ago—talking of life and lions and watching the white moon shed her cool light over the dark trees and bushes. The lamp on the table burned bright and painted around us a warm, friendly golden circle.

Can we ever be quite the same? Can we ever erase from our minds the memory of the love and the trust between us and the lions, and the betrayal of the trust? I think not. As I sit in my room and hear the cold wind beating on the window I think of our lions in their zoos—does that same wind whistle round their cages and chill their hearts?

As we, in growing older, remember the past—its joys, sorrows, fulfilments and disappointments—do these caged lions think back often to their walks on the sunlit plains, to their patient hours of stalking game through the bush, to their happy splashing in the rivers and dams and well-earned rest in the shade of the thorn trees? This is a part of the free and natural life that George Adamson could have helped them to lead, but now is lost to them for ever.